D ❋ Dawn

AND OTHER POEMS

D*DAWN

AND OTHER POEMS

By

Margaret McGarvey

Privately Printed
FOR
THE McGARVEY FAMILY
°
THE ASHANTILLY PRESS
DARIEN, GEORGIA
MCMLXIV

Dedication

ONE day in 1927, a notice appeared in The *Savannah Morning News* of a contest sponsored by the PoetrySociety of Georgia, the judge to be Edward Davidson, an editor of The *Saturday Review of Literature*. Margaret McGarvey entered a poem in this contest and while she did not win first place, she received such warm praise and encouragement from the judge that her literary ideals came ablaze again. Nothing must do but she must join the Poetry Society.

❡ The high standards of the Poetry Society, its instruction, guidance, competitions and awards were to give back to her the incentive to write seriously which had been inhibited by circumstances and environment. Membership brought rewarding friendships which were to continue throughout her life.

❡ Therefore, it is with gratitude that this book, printed posthumously, is dedicated to the Poetry Society of Georgia, whose existence made possible these poems and the poems of many another Georgia writer.

Table of Contents

❈❈❈❈❈❈❈❈❈❈❈❈❈❈❈❈❈❈❈❈❈❈❈❈❈❈❈

Acknowledgments

❊

THE family of Margaret McGarvey wish to express their appreciation to the following publications and associations for permitting the reprinting of her poems in this volume in memory of the writer: *

   The Los Angeles Examiner, The New York Herald
Tribune, The New York Sun, The New York Times;
The Saturday Evening Post, The Saturday Review Of
Literature, Spirit, The Stratford Magazine,
Versecraft (The Banner Press), American Women Poets,
Manuscript and Columbia Poetry (both by the Columbia
University Press); Georgia Writers Conference,
The Poetry Society of South Carolina, The Poetry
Society of Georgia.

*

Any proceeds from the sale of this book will be used to provide prizes for poetry.

 *Awards and publication credits for the individual poems
are listed on the subtitle page immediately preceding
the group of poems to which they refer.*

Foreword

BECAUSE I believe that the poems of Margaret McGarvey represent an achievement far surpassing that of a mere clever artist, it is a privilege for me to recommend unreservedly her work to the discerning and discriminating reader.

Among the qualities of this gifted poet are mastery of technique, maturity of thought, vividness of imagery, artistic restraint. On every page will be found evidences of a wild yet controlled imagination, deep and massive powers of feeling, felicity of vision and of expression. Above all other virtues, perhaps, in this singer, is a lonely and lovely originality.

This is high praise. That it is merited the reader may prove for himself. Let him but read such magical poems as *Perception, Obit, Barter, The Dreamer* (and many others), and he will at once be aware that he is listening to a new Voice, starry and authentic, singing of the ancient trinity of Life, Love, and Death.

There is sorrow in this book; but it is more cosmic than personal; and I believe that to shed those tears of eternity that fall for all humanity requires an especial gallantry of heart, an especial tenderness and genuineness of perception, and of response to that perception.

I have deeply felt, and I believe that every reader of this beautiful book will feel that these poems have about them the air of immortality. That air can never be feigned; and its effect on the human spirit is inevitable — flooding that spirit with celestial light, and filling it with gratitude, with wonder, with awe, and with the rapture that glorious song alone can give.

Archibald Rutledge

McClellanville, South Carolina
14 February, 1951

 ❋ Dawn

D ☆ *DAWN*, Spirit, a Magazine of Poetry.

THE TRAGIC TOY, The Seymour Prize,
Judge: Robert Tristram Coffin, (Year Book Poetry Society
of Georgia).

THIS WAS IN WILDER WEATHER,
First Place, Poetry Society of Georgia.

THE LOST HAMLET, The Sonnet Prize, Georgia
Writers' Conference.

JUNE SIXTH, 1944:
The commander of a U. S. base in England said to his airmen: "May I
have your attention, please? This is what we have been waiting for. This
is invasion morning." His young men went out to their planes and up
into the Channel dawn. TIME ; issue of June 12, 1944.

✩

FATHER, sitting on the side of your startled bed,
   May I have your attention, please?
This is not the morning you stopped short in a corridor
And thanked God on your knees.

> *The hospital walls dissolve in joy,*
> *The sun shouts as it rises:*
> *"The Johnsons have an eight pound boy*
> *Exceeding all surmises!"....*

Morning comes early when a child is small—
A nudge from Heaven or a sparrow's cheep,
And he is off to find a dreamed-of ball
Rolled to him down the corridors of sleep....

> Has Santy come yet?
> *No, Dear, not quite.*
> (Shall we let him go in?
> *Wait till it's lit.)...*
> You saw him yourself?
> What was he like?
> Did he really bring me
> A big boy's bike?...
> *No, Dear, not Christmas—*
> *But the day selected*
> *For you to be brave—*
> *Braver than expected!*

Mother, still awake when the frightened whistles blew,
This is not the morning of the Boy Scout Hike.
Lie still, lie still, there's nothing you can do
Except to pray a while if you should like.

The bedroom walls dissolve in pain,
The sun shrieks as it rises:
"The Johnson boy's in danger now
Exceeding all surmises!...

He sprints across the still-cool lawn,
Behavior sewn upon his chest;
A skinny, brown and freckled fawn
Who's passed the Scouts' initial test....

Mom, if I'd a needle
And some coarse thread,
I could sew it on
Like I saw Fred.
Mother will sew it, Don
Mother will press it....
Does it hurt much?
Mother will dress it....
Mother will die for you —
(You know that is true.)
Now, Mom, that's something
YOU NO CAN DO!

Young Man, waiting in the pale Channel dawn,
Waiting at attention for the signal to fly,
This is the morning for which you were born,
This is the morning on which you shall die.

> *The shores of home dissolve in mist,*
> *The sun booms as it rises:*
> *"The Johnsons have a hero now*
> *Exceeding all surmises."*

Morning comes early when a child is gone —
(Surely by now his plane is in the sky.)
Will he take cold there in the Channel dawn?
Will he be lonely when he comes to die?...

> This is not the morning
> Of the Sunday-School Picnic.
> This is not the morning
> Don gets his degree.
> This is not the morning
> He might up and marry
> Betty Ann Smith
> Or Little Nancy Lee —
> Nor is it the morning
> You lit his First Tree....
> This is the morning
> For which we've been waiting,
> This is the morning
> Of praying and hating —
> This is Invasion Morning!

The Tragic Toy

THE sea he loved as a tiny boy
Was never more than a gigantic toy —
   A shining toy which his black nurse wound
   Summer-long near Simon's Sound.

The beach was the sill of the sea's blue door,
Nurse turned a knob and the sea would roar.
   She made pipers skim and small boats rock,
   And sea gulls wheel in a tidy flock…

Later Father (who better could know?)
Said the sea was a plaything he'd not outgrow.
   He would love it always as he had done —
   Sea for father and sea for son.

But Father's sea was a summer tide,
Silken-green and warm and wide;
   Or a blue fall day in a grass-caught creek
   With the only prey a marsh hen's beak…

The only prey, and now his son
The hunter and hunted adrift as one.
   No grass to clutch but dark and wide
   The heaving weight of a winter tide….

Years from the Sound and miles from shore,
But he heard the sea that Nurse made roar,
   And the blue door opened — misty, wide —,
   A tired child, he crept inside.

THE sea was forever reaching
   To take what we might own —
Its greedy, restless fingers
   Picked us like a bone.

Yet, in the hurricane weather,
   My son and I would chance
To walk the battered beaches
   And watch the tide's advance;

To watch the Light's dim wheeling,
   The Island lost in spray;
The trees and houses reeling
   As roots were swept away...

The sea was forever reaching
   To take what I might own,
And then its thieving fingers
   Cleaned me to the bone!

Took from me forever
   What it never touched before —
But this was in wilder weather —
   This was the weather of war!

The Lost Hamlet

AFTER a while the heart went out of the people,
　　They no longer danced in the village square;
　　Their faces forgot to shine like the town's one steeple,
　　Their children grew sickly, their beasts were too spare.
　　For bewilderment shatters the stoutest will
　　When pitchfork nor spade can set things to right:
　　The wolf in the fold? Yes, but people the kill,
　　And the stony road closed that once offered flight.
　　Before terror struck and when haying was done
　　(Their children brisk parents of six or of seven),
　　Old couples would gladly leave work in the sun
　　To prepare for their own modest journeys to heaven.
　　But no one can fathom nor does history tell
　　Why such gentle hamlets should fall into hell.

 hough years have sped

THE BALLAD OF EBO, The Barrow Prize, Poetry
Society of Georgia, for the best ballad on American history.
Judge: Martha Keller (Yr. Bk. P. S. of Georgia).

THE FANS, The Beatrice Allen Igoe Memorial Prize, for a
ballad, Poetry Society of South Carolina (Yr. Bk. P. S. of South
Carolina).

HOMECOMING, The Popular Prize, Poetry Society of
Georgia, (Yr. Bk. P. S. of Georgia).

DOWN AT DE WHARF, Columbia Poetry,
Columbia University Press.

On the west shore of St. Simons Island, Georgia, almost opposite Twitty Park, is a bluff known as Ebo Landing, where slave ships used to land their human cargoes and hold them in camps until they were sold. Rather than submit to a life of servitude, a group of Africans of the Ebo tribe, who were encamped there, marched into the water and were drowned. To this day, no Negro fisherman on St. Simons Island will drop a hook at Ebo.

From Our Todays and Yesterdays
By Margaret Davis Cate

☆

AT Ebo Landing, though years have sped,
The waters speak with the voice of the dead.
 Those waters heave and those waters moan,
 And no one's going there alone!
 (Two might go but never alone)...

In eighteen hundred and forty-two,
A slave ship steered by Aaron Blue,
 Brought to Georgia as contraband
 One hundred slaves and an extra hand.

The extra hand was a fulah chief,
Tall with pride and gaunt with grief
(Smouldering, sullen sort of grief),
 Whose shackled subjects still would do
 Whatever their leader told them to...

At St. Simons Island Blue dropped anchor
With the sulky slaves and the Fulah rancor;
 Released their fetters but not their yokes,
 Encamped his herd mid the great live oaks...

The earth seemed heaven after the hold
Of the filthy ship to the dusky fold,
    To all save Ebo, the princely one
    Who refused to smile in the Georgia sun;

Who refused to face a bondsman's doom
But moped instead in the live oak gloom,
    Or beset his subjects with the plea
    That they escape in the nearby sea.

But slave ships bring and never take,
And there's no cure for slaves' heartache,
    So they asked of Ebo, where could they go,
    Where in this new world could poor slaves go?

"The waters brought us, they'll take us back!"
(His words fell sharp like a thunder-crack)
    So no one questioned the princely one,
    Though the slaves felt free in the Georgia sun...

For there were the waters waiting and ready,
And to pine for home is an ache that's steady —
    An ache that's steady for those who lack
    And surely the waters would take them back!...

The spring woods stirred with the stealthy sound
Of dark feet treading the spongy ground,
    Of bare feet leaving the Georgia loam,
    For Ebo's people were going home...

The island hounds sniffed the fragrant air,
Their eager baying was everywhere,
    But Ebo had led his barefoot crew
    To promised freedom — a stretch of blue.

☆   ☆   ☆

At Ebo Landing, though years have sped,
The waters speak with the voice of the dead.
    The waters speak as dusky throats,
    And this is the burden of their notes:

"The waters bring and the waters take,
"And the sea's a cure for dark heartache —
"The only cure for slaves' heartbreak."

The Fans

A BALLAD OF RECONSTRUCTION DAYS IN
BEAUFORT, SOUTH CAROLINA

"THESE are things from Beaufort," so Aunt Carrie said,
Bringing cardboard boxes down the attic stair,
Lifting decades of defeat from their battered care.

A girdle deftly stitched by hand, an apron for a child,
Trimmings from the trousseau of a long-dead bride;
Clippings from the *Courier*— yellowed print of pride.

"These are just some odds and ends, nothing that is fine,
General Sherman never left very much behind,
Nothing that my saving aunts would pay half a mind..."

But there was another box — shallow, wide, and square —
And what seemed a living thing lay within it there,
And what seemed a heron's wing drooped for lack of air.

"Did I ever tell you," my Aunt Carrie smiled,
As she lifted up that thing, dazzling white and mild,
"That my aunts made fans of wings when I was a child?"

"Oh, how cruel," I shuddered, how was I to know
That the bread those great-aunts ate came from herons' snow,
That the calicoes they wore were a bird's quick woe;

That the black boys brought them in, limp and dripping white,
From the Carolina coast in the early light,
So the neighbors wouldn't know of their desperate plight?

☆　　☆　　☆

"But sea-gull fans were loveliest," my Aunt Carrie said,
"Brought a better price, of course, and *pink* sea gulls were rare;
Sea gull feathers had to be handled with real care."

"Haven't you a sea gull one?"— surely there must be
Pinioned somewhere in that pile one that I could see —
"No one kept a sea-gull fan that I know," said she...

What emotions one could fan with a sea gull's wing,
Surely, then, the dullest breast must take heart and sing!
But no one kept a sea-gull fan — did they, then, take wing?

Did they fly from too much life in a fragrant room,
Flee a casual, jeweled hand for the sea's wild gloom,
Seek its trackless wastes of gray as a better doom?

☆   ☆   ☆

No one kept a sea-gull fan from that pensive place,
Where the world was seen through moss tenuous as lace,
And the black boys in the marsh stopped a bird's swift race;

Where unflinching ladies rose sadly in defeat,
Made a living that they kept nameless and discreet —
Fashioned fans of dazzling wings for the world's élite.

LIMNED by the sunset's pencils,
These dusky ones might be
The servants of the sultan
Or pirates from the sea.

Their arms and backs bear riches,
Their heads are burden-proud,
But not from Istanbul's bazaars
Returns this straggling crowd.

These are but Georgia Negroes
Bowed down at end of day
With all the blessings that the Lord
Has scattered on their way:

Gray moss to make a mattress,
Flung from a wind-blown oak;
Some cotton snips and rosin chips
To make a sand-fly smoke.

A coffee can of ham grease
(The white folks couldn't use);
A broken dish, a string of fish,
A pair of cast-off shoes.

Limp bundles of old papers
To hang up in the shack;
Some faded gimp and scarlet shrimp,
A melon with a crack.

One pulls a whining wagon
Made from a packing case;
And crocus sacks on ragged backs
Swell with unconscious grace.

A toothless crone bears branches,
Oh, blesséd wind and rain,
You rent the oak that flame and smoke
Might dance for old Mom Jane!

They pass with easy laughter,
Their heads held burden-high,
The heirs of all god's debris
Beneath the Georgia sky.

Down at de wharf

DOWN at de wharf dere's a big ship in,
Got a smoke-stack black as de Debbil's sin,
Got a whistle loud as a jubilee,
It blow an' blow but it warn't fer me —
Down at de wharf dis mawnin'.

I goes down early, de sky plum black,
Mought jes' es well stay in mah shack,
Fer all I does is ter wear out shoes,
An' hangs aroun' an' hears bad news —
Down at de wharf dis mawin'.

Oh, we rolls dat rosin no mo,' no mo',
We rolls dat rosin no mo'.
De ships come in as dey done befo'
But we rolls dat rosin no mo'.

De sun come out an' de sun go in,
Us hangs aroun' in de cole an' win'.
Jes' hangs aroun' an' talk 'bout how
De "w'ite meat" fer de w'ite folks now —
Down at de wharf dis mawnin'.

I dream dere warn't no cranes an' t'ings
Ter fetch dat rosin lak it bohn wid wings;
Dream we rolls it till de moon comes out,
An' all-us niggers jes sweat an' shout —
But I wakes up in de mawnin'.

Oh, we rolls dat rosin no mo', no mo',
We rolls dat rosin no mo'.
De whistle blow at ha'pas' t'ree,
It blow an' blow but it warn't fer me,
(No, Lawd, it warn't fer me) —
Down at de wharf dis mawnin'.

 *flexure of foam*

THE BULLS OF SEA ISLAND, Columbia Poetry,
Columbia University Press.

BARTER, The Seymour Prize, Judge: William Rose Benet,
Poetry Society of Georgia.

MARSH MATERNAL, Versecraft, Banner Press.

THE mad blue bulls of Sea Island
    That are driven by the moon,
Have broken away from their traces
    And plunged into afternoon.

They are roaming the pale gold beaches,
    They are stamping the shining sand,
They are horning the tawny bathers,
    And tossing them back to land.

Rejoice with your sons and daughters
    When the mad blue bulls are a-roam,
For their flanks are a ripple of waters,
    Their horns are a flexure of foam.

Though they scoop up your sons like seaweed,
    Though they shake your gold daughters in sport,
Though they lift up your beautiful children
    And toss them aside with a snort,

Exult with your sons and daughters
    For where is the mortal who scorns
To be one with the shining waters
    And tossed on the foaming horns!

Barter

ASK the sea for pity,
  Try not to care
If all you get
  Is a cold-blue stare.

It's much too busy
  With cargo and crew,
Tides and turnings
  To be sorry for you.

It sucks your ships
  And breaks your will,
And leaves on the beach
  A sea gull's quill.

It sends your son
  To a watery hell,
But all you find
  In the sand is a shell.

A wave-tossed shell
  For his beautiful youth—
No sea chantey this
  But a sea-bitten truth.

Shout out your sorrow,
  The sea won't listen,
Deep in the dusk
  It will slide and glisten.

Glisten with stars,
   Slide over your loss,
And leave in your life
   A mariner's cross....

It will break your heart
   (It did that for me)....
Lord, how I hate
   To love the sea!

*W*HAT hunted things a marsh can hide
In her pockets green and wide!
   If you wish poor creatures well,
   Never tell, oh, never tell
Of the marsh hens, snipe and coots
Sheltered in her watery shoots;
   Of the heron's boggy bower
   Fast as any fabled tower.

What vestal things a marsh can hold
In her lap of reedy gold:
   Mollusks curled within a shell,
   Fearful of the ocean's swell;
And on alabaster wings,
Whitest of all virgin things,
   There the heron steals away
   From the stare of lustful day.

What secret flights a marsh can keep
In her breasts so dark and deep....
   If you would not break a spell,
   Never tell, oh, never tell
Of the heron's ghostly rise
To the waiting sunset skys,—
   Of her lonely twilight tryst
   When the marsh is clothed in mist.

old leaf frames on famous people

DAPHNE, Year Book Poetry Society of South Carolina, set to music.

OBIT, F. P. A.'s Conning Tower, The New York Herald Tribune.

AT ASTOLAT, First place, Poetry Society of Georgia.

PORTUGUESE FISHERMAN, Columbia Poetry, Columbia University Press.

AUNT JANIE, American Women Poets, Edited by Margery Mansfield.

SKIPPER MICK, Columbia Poetry, Columbia University Press.

TWO SPINSTERS ON A MATERNITY FLOOR, Unpublished.

Continued over leaf

DILETTANTE, The Epigram Prize, Poetry Society of Georgia (Yr. Bk. P. S. of Georgia).

ACCESSORY, Honorable Mention, Poetry Society of Georgia.

THE MIRACLE, The Society Prize, Poetry Society of Georgia, Judge: B. Y. Williams (Yr. Bk. P. S. of Georgia).

THE COMFORTER, First Place, Poetry Society of Georgia.

AUDITION, The Critics Prize, Poetry Society of Georgia.

DAFFODILS and yellow dishes,
  Amber beads and golden fishes,
    Resin from the southern pine,
    Lambent flame and candle-shine;
  Tulip in a saffron smock,
  Poppy in a golden frock,
    Burnished brasses, butterflies;
    Halos, moons, and tigers' eyes;
  Golden globes of citrus fruit,
  Dripping honey— bee hives' loot,
    Gold-leaf frames on famous people,
    Sun-dawn on a Gothic steeple;
  Miser's money— hard and bright,
  Star-bloom in a dusky night,
    Tawny wheat in shaggy sheaves,
    And the alchemy of leaves—
  Nothing, nothing can compare
  With the color of your hair!

Obit

SHE painted leather for his chair,
  And put in base-plugs everywhere.
    Two layers of curtains hid the view,
    And Parrish pictures made things blue.

She said her purpose was to make
  "A homing spot for his dear sake."...
    He feared a "cozy" grave and so
    He chose the ocean's undertow.

At Astolat

(*Elaine meditates — Lancelot tarries*)

HIS armor stands empty
　　And I am at peace
　For the tempest outside
　　Refuses to cease.

　The ivy is wrenched
　　From the tower room wall;
　Below the wind's wailing
　　The aspen trees fall.

　The lightning leaps lilac
　　Across the black sky;
　The rain hisses madly,
　　And downy things die.

　My loom knows no weaving,
　　The light is too dim
　To see anything
　　But the pale face of him.

　The wind is too loud
　　With its moan and its mutter,
　To hear anything
　　But words he might utter.

　The rains that have swollen
　　The brooks and the river
　Have dampened these walls
　　So the strongest must shiver.

But his armor stands empty
    Like an ominous cage—
Great God in your mercy
    Let the storm rage!

Portuguese Fisherman

*H*IS rosary redolent of fish
    Is twined about his horny hand,
With candles, coffin, Sunday suit
    He's anchored to an alien land.

All sea-roads led to Portugal
    And so he'd known beyond a doubt
That Georgia was no place to die
    But to command the price of trout!

From door to door he cried his wares,
    Nor found the city streets too narrow,
Because he wheeled the sea about
    Like supple silver in his barrow....

Now he who held his palm-strung catch
    To charm the housewife's Friday eye,
Cannot leap out of Death's dark net
    Back to the friendly sea to die!

*J*N summer, in winter, she knocks on our door,
Aunt Janie who says she's one hundred and more.
Though a film veils the eyes that saw General Lee,
And her black body's bent like a storm-twisted tree,
From each awkward step some strange grace is flowing,
She says it's the Lord that keeps her a-going.
　And maybe it is, for each morning at mass
　When the sanctus bell rings down the aisle she will pass....

With the taste of the Lord still sweet in her mouth,
She knocks on our door in rainspell or drouth,
　And her voice is as soft as a magnolia petal
　When she asks for a sip from our late-boiling kettle....

Aunt Janie's a virgin, she was to have wed
But her lover was sold down the river it's said,
Though her master was kind and so proud of his French,
That she sips café noir on our little porch bench.
He owned a whole island, raised rice, hell and cotton,
Mulberry trees and things she's forgotten,
But she praises his swearing and remembers Miss Val,
The daughter who died—"Sech a lively young gal"—;
His son who was killed , his "nigger" named Moses;
His gentle wife's passion for Cherokee roses,
　And a century's lost petals are strewn down our walk
　When Aunt Janie's "mis'ry" permits her to talk.

She carries a basket, she leans on her stick,
She's one hundred and more and never bed-sick.
Her hands are like twigs, gnarled, black, and a-quiver,
Her massive feet move like rafts on a river,
　But from each awkward step some strange grace is flowing,
　She says it's the Lord that keeps her a-going.

Skipper Mick

(From an Irish Painting by Robert Henri)

STURDY, I call it, to stand so straight
For the painter chap and you but eight!
Just like a skipper he painted you, too,
With stout green reefer and cap askew;
The crimson kerchief tied seamanwise,
The stubby hair and the Celtic eyes.
I could almost see you commanding ships
If 'twere not for the childish full red lips....
But didn't you want to leave and run
Out on the moor with the wind and sun,
Tagging at heel a reckless dog,
Chasing rabbits through field and bog?
And didn't you want to stop and gather
A bit of may or a smell of heather;
Climb the steeps where the four winds blow,
And the highway creeps a mile below,
Upon the warm gray ledge to lie
And watch the castle folk go by;
See the sunlight gild the steeple,
And think upon the Little People?...
How can I tell you would act just so?
Oh, Skipper Mick, could I help but know,
With my own dead father once as small
And a tike like yourself in Donegal!

Two Spinsters on a maternity floor

NO slight intended, understand,
    That all they get is life's cold shoulder.
    They watch through plate-glass rows of babes
      And feel a thousand years or older.

Bearers of presents, wrapped in blue
    For Mary's son, who's such a whopper,
    And wrapped in pink for Jennie's girl,
      A bottle with a new type stopper.

This is their only business here—
    To make glad sounds for others joy:
    "So glad that Jennie has a girl,
      So glad that Mary has a boy!"

Their cups will never now run over,
    Past is the time of foolish maybe,
    So they remark as they descend:
      "It's awfully warm to have a baby."

Dilettante

HE dabbled some in all the arts
    With ardor undiminished;
    Here lies his body quite complete—
    The only thing he finished.

*J*N the papers that I read,
  People freeze and burn and and bleed;
  Daily, with the enriched toast,
  They give up their tragic ghost,
  And I do not even blink
  At murder done in printer's ink...

  But when they found him dead today—
  One who often passed my way—,
  A man so spare with what he said,
  He never spoke but bowed his head—
  One so lavish with his breath,
  He did not wait but sent for death,

  I needed no reporter's art
  To see his stiff hand on his heart—
  A heart so overcharged with woe,
  He could not wait his time to go
  But chose it with deliberate care
  As one who buys a pullman fare!

  To see the dingy, rented room,
  The bedside table like a doom
  That held the glass, release from life
  Which brought no pulsing child or wife
  To him, who, heedful of the spread,
  Died gingerly upon the bed...

  Though this man barely spoke to me,
  Yet of his death I am not free.
  He who in life encroached on none,
  Beside me now a place has won—
  As if we had a lifelong pact,
  I have become part of his act.

The Miracle

I MET my mother on the street today
   And thought how strange it was to see her there,
With glove-clutched bag and hat of genteel gray
   Perched carefully upon her straying hair.

The traffic's hum went on at impious pitch,
   The never ending people up and down,
And yet a household saint had fled her niche
   To make her anxious, jostled way to town!

How odd this dear familiar sight to see,
   As if an errant dove flocked with the crows,
Or down the pathway strolled our dogwood tree,
   Or from the trellis climbed the clinging rose.

In city streets such miracles are rare —
I never shall forget I met her there.

THE comforter sits in the midst of despair,
  Not too relaxed but cheerful withal,
For soon she may rise from the petit point chair
  And put on her mouton wrap in the hall.

Soon she may check from her handbag list,
  Among things to buy at the ten cents store,
This visit that made her pale eyes mist
  As death was told in the room once more.

She thinks with relief of the undistressed,
  Of matters little concerned with the dead,
And all of the while from east to west
  Her world is toppling about her head!

YOU feel she has said at the thought of disaster,
  "If it happened to me there'd still be my singing,"
And she's preened at the thought of this nebulous calling,
So easy it is in a dream to unfasten
The cage of the throat and set a song winging,
While the rain of applause is steadily falling.

So easy it is, but now she is standing
With hands tightly shut to keep them from shaking,
Defending her right to this dream she's been hoarding,
This beautiful dream that was never demanding
But flowered the night and eased the awaking
Of one to whom life has been clerking and boarding.

She could have had such delight in her keeping
For many a moon, but its beauty is waning
With the first flurry of notes bravely flying...
Oh, a dream that is lost is no cause for weeping —
Should blossoms appear when winter is reigning,
Or song still ascend when one's youth is dying?

 *ake room for the flowers*

OYEZ, *The Monthly Prize, Poetry Society of Georgia (Yr. Bk. P. S. of Georgia).*

HALLS, *Unpublished.*

HYDRANGEAS, *The Saturday Review of Literature.*

WHITE WISTERIA, *The Jackson Prize, Poetry Society of Georgia, set to music.*

THE UNSOUGHT BEAUTY, *Columbia Poetry, Columbia University Press, under name of "Spent Beauty."*

THE UNKNOWN FLOWER, *Honorable Mention, Poetry Society of South Carolina.*

IN AUGUST, *Los Angeles Examiner.*

HUNTRESS, *Year Book, Poetry Society of Georgia.*

Oyez

IN the gray garden
 The frozen earth swells
For little green criers
 Are ringing white bells—
Proclaiming arrival
 Of colors and smells.

"Make room for the flowers,
 Make room, make room,"
The white bells peal
 In the garden's gloom—
Ten thousand snowdrops
 Heralding bloom.

Halls

COOL corridors of opal
 That lead where no one knows,
With tapestries of purple
And oriels of rose.

Where are these halls of faery?
Whose dream, or in what story?
*Long, long ago I found my way
Into a morning glory.*

Hydrangeas

MISS Anna's hydrangeas
    Are banquets of bloom.
Drink deep of the blueness
    Set forth in this room.

And think of a garden,
    A house of gray lace,
And the bloom of hydrangeas
    That tented the place.

All woven of water,
    Of fragrance and fay—
Pagodas by evening,
    Umbrellas by day,

Think back to school-closings
    At dusk in the town,
Of urns of hydrangeas
    And Mary's white gown....

Gone now is Miss Anna,
    Gone now the green hand
That loosened the earth
    To flower her land.

Yet still the hydrangeas
    Are banquets of bloom.
Drink deep of the blueness
    Set forth in this room.

J DREAMED of white wisteria
  In dark lanes of the oak.
  It crept up in the brooding tree,
  On vine-feet crept it stealthily,
  And then its pale lips spoke:
  In fragrant frost on every branch,
  A startling, snowy avalanche
  That lit the ancient oak....
  But while its coming still was glowing,
  It spoke in syllables of going,
  And crept from out that loving tree,
  Yet crept away so stealthily
  No watch dog woke.
  And no one marked its ghostly going,
  Only that radiance ceased flowing—
  For what could there be eerier
  Than speech of white wisteria
  In dark lanes of the oak?

The unsought beauty

*T*O lovely maids one needs no guide;
    And so without a map or chart,
  Men found the bloom she could not hide
    And set her radiance apart.

Yet far away, lost in a wood,
    So still and deep it seemed a doom,
A tree in bridal whiteness stood
    And flowered in the twilight gloom.

"IT'S white ageratum," Elsbeth said,
  "Look at the leaves and its powdery head."
"It's plain sea myrtle," from final Flo,
"After Botany 30 I should know."
"The terminal cymes are shaped like a cup;"
So Alice thought they should look it up.

With flowering arms they left the wood
Where the nameless scribbled its livelihood;
Thrust its roots in the blackest earth
And scattered rhymes of a snowy mirth,—
Rhymes and runes and pale quatrains
Till the dark woods whitened with its refrains.

Came deeper dusks and the languid leaf,
And the nameless knew that its stay was brief,
But still it wrote with its reckless roots
Songs as lovely as those from flutes,—
Songs that blossomed with no one knowing
Of whence they came or their ghostly going.

NO, the roses are gone,
>   Did you think when you came
>   You would find them still kindling
>   Pale amber and flame?
>   Return to a garden,
>   It's never the same.

The midsummer heat
Put the lilies to route,
Like stars in the dawn
The daisies went out,
And the zinnias are parched
Because of the drought.

I miss them, of course,
But why contemplate flight
When a garden can yield
Even dearer delight —
The wind in the trees
And your voice in the night.

APRIL'S a huntress dressed in green,
  Riding the earth with a sportive mien.
  Follow the trail and you will see
  Flicks of her crop on bush and tree...
  One clear note from a birdlike horn
  Hastens the limpid steps of dawn,
  Wakens the pack of leashed desires—
  Whelps and dams and lean gray sires.
    Hunting blood—all winter pent—
    Sniffing the trail of jasmine scent.

April's a huntress keen for the chase,
  Riding the earth with a subtle grace.
  Her quiver's the sky, her spurs the sun,
  And of new-green leaf is her habit spun...
  She cracks her whip in copse and wood,
  For the chase is merry, the quarry good.
  With fine sure aim and sportsman ease
  She shatters the bloom of pregnant trees.
    Oh, deep the wound and keen the pain
    Of argent arrows of the rain!

April's a huntress content to rest
  After the ardor of her quest.
  Trotting along at a gentle pace,
  Sunset staining her wistful face...
  High in the spacious halls of night
  She hangs her quarry in full sight.
  Sometimes she bags a million stars,
  A planet or so, like the wary Mars...
    But sweet the song and blithe the tune
    When April bags the foxy moon!

nd all the pretty trifles

THE DEBTORS, The New York Times.

THE STRANGER, Manuscript, Columbia University Press.

FIREWORKS, The New York Times.

DETOUR, The New York Sun.

WHO sees a tree in blossom,
    Or in its time of leaf,
Dares not to think such loveliness
    Shall some day come to grief....
"We must be gay in April"
    Laugh slender, girlish trees,
And so they order fragrance
    Or petals as they please.
They reckon not on Autumn
    When mists hang on the hill,
And the Shylock wind comes creaking
    To collect his careful bill....

The golden leaves are twirling
    Upon the dusty ground
To pay for light rain patter—
    That fragile April sound—;
For stretches of pale petals,
    The flitting of a wing,
And all the pretty trifles
    Trees fancy in the spring.
The yellow leaves are drifting
    Since trees must pay for all—
The stars they fasten in their boughs,
    The robin's mating call....

The Shylock wind is counting
    The gold leaves in his till,
And slender trees are shivering—
    Stark nakéd on the hill.

A STRANGER sought my house last night,
    Last night, late, when the moon was thin.
His gestures told of sudden flight —
    Naught to do but let him in.

The wind was fragrant on the lawn,
    The garden path was white as day,
And soon would stir the sleeping dawn,
    But out of doors he would not stay.

So to my room of shabby things
    The vivid stranger came to rest;
His robes were rich as those of kings
    Upon some mediaeval quest.

His cloak so proudly worked with crewels,
    Was silver tissue — fold on fold;
Some cunning smith with precious jewels
    Had set his diadem of gold....

A stranger died in here last night,
    And now there lies upon the cloth —
The broken wings of frantic flight,
    The crumpled beauty of a moth.

AFTER the town's heat-fretted day
We found the beach-drive cool with spray,
Cool with spray and wet with foam
The breakers left as they scurried home.
We hailed the first star's feeble twinkle
Above the ocean's silken wrinkle,
And loved in duskiness anew
The shrinking sea, its faint tattoo....
Then someone flung across the black—
Tall topaz trees, a golden track,
A fountain spray, a flock of stars,
And gems once favored by the Tsars.
Intent upon this magic light,
We marveled with a fresh delight
That paper cylinders could hold
Such miracles of green and gold,
And beauty's dictum could survive
The playthings that mere men contrive—
A Roman candle's sparkling rush,
Or else a rocket's astral gush.

WE were in haste but could not pass
  A purple flare of feather grass.
    Though sloth that day could be but blunder,
    We stopped our car and gazed in wonder
  At floating fans of gauzy shoots
  As if bright birds had taken roots....

Tart time has etched that heady sip
  In sharper acid than our trip.
    We were in haste but can't recall
    The destination now at all.
  To that dim goal we can not pass—
  The way is choked with feather grass.

 *ransports*

TRANSPORTS, First Place, Poetry Society of Georgia.

THE FIRE, The New York Herald Tribune.

HEAT, The Saturday Evening Post.

TRANSITION, The Society Prize, Poetry Society of South Carolina.

IN THE PINE LANDS, Hercules Mixer.

Transports

WHERE the land is lapped by the sea,
    We stopped on the edge of day
And remarked on a cargo of light
    That was stored in the silent bay.

No stevedore came forward
    To load that precious stuff,
Nor was there ship to carry,
    Or wind and tide enough.

But even while we lingered,
    As sudden as miracles,
There came a sweeping of wings
    And the bay was filled with gulls...

Like transports limned in gold,
    We watched them seaward borne;
And as we turned in the dusk,
    The cargo of light was gone.

The Fire

THROW on the oak and sycamore,
    Last summer's shade and autumn's boast;
Throw on the cedar and wild plum,
    December's cheer and April's ghost;
Pile on the boughs that sheltered once
    The mockingbirds and their slight nest—
      We must give all to keep with us
      This crackling, rude, and ruddy guest!

Heat

HEAT holds the lowlands now
In its hot embrace,
Gives the hungry piney-folk
Little cause for grace.

Women lean all languid-like
In the open door,
Nakéd children, puppy-wise,
Sprawl upon the floor.

Heat holds the scraggy patch
Up to farming scorn,
Turns to tawny paper scraps
Rows of young green corn.

Strips the idling men-folk down
To hairy chest and breeches,
Leaves the bony cows to thirst
At the dried-up ditches....

In the shimmering haze of heat
Only buzzards pass,
Soar above an August world
Still as under glass.

NOT the dropping of nuts,
   The drifting of leaves,
   Complaints from the pigeons
   In rain-sodden eaves;
   The mists in the morning,
   The swallows' wise flight,
   The dahlias' stiff blooming,
   The edge of the night;
   The grasses' slow turning
   From emerald to fawn,
     Convey to my senses
     That summer is gone.

But here on the highway
This blown yellow thing,
Much brighter than amber,
A butterfly's wing—
Propeller of joy
In roses and clover—
   Proclaims by its stillness
   That summer is over.

In the Pine Lands

HOW did I know
   As I came through the wood
   That though sterile the soil
   The yield would be good?

In the rose dusk the stretch
Of ascending black lines
Gave no hope of new life
In the fire-scarred pines.

How dusty the path,
How thirsty the corn;
No gentle rain spoke,
The grass was still-born.

The katydids chirped
And little pigs grunted —
Above me arose
Life arid and stunted...

But a star beckoned on
Where the cabin smoke curled —
Though sterile the land
How rich was my world

Since ruby-like glowed
In the dusk of the clearing
The lamplight that led
To the end of despairing!

For how could I doubt
That earth would renew,
When barren pine plains
Yielded promise of you?

ass for the Dead

ALL SOULS DAY; MASS FOR THE DEAD,
Columbia Poetry, Columbia University Press.

FOR EVENING, Columbia Poetry, Columbia University
Press.

THE CAMEL, The Stratford Magazine, Boston Massa-
chusetts.

PERCEPTION, The Jackson Prize, Poetry Society of
Georgia, set to music.

THE LOST ONE, Columbia Poetry, Columbia Uni-
versity Press.

BIRD SONG, Unpublished.

*T*HIS is the first mass of the day
  And worshippers will be but few.
The church is dim with dawn and fog,
  Grope on to find your pew.

My pew is taken, so is yours!
  See, everyone is occupied,
With people crowding in the back
  And standing up along the side!

How odd that tourists should be here,
  The morning's much too dark for travel,
Yet still they come in from the street,
  Their footsteps light upon the gravel....

The alter candles lick the gloom
  Persistently with tongues of flame —
These are not tourists kneeling here,
  I know these people all by name!

There's Shiela Clay, whom Clyde adored,
  She afterwards was Andrew's wife;
I always liked her best in blue —
  She's just as lovely as in life!

And Manuel Cross, who sold us fish,
  And flourished gaily during Lent;
He never brought us that last string —
  It was Friday that he went.

Poor Sally of the leaking heart —
  For once her cheeks are really pink!
And Charlie Bates, who clerked in Sparks —
  Proud, still, of his sardonic wink.

Across the aisle, free as the air,
   Kneels Agnes, who was "put away"
Because she mumbled all the time —
   How calmly she has learned to pray!

They all are calm, these pleasant ghosts;
   Unhurried in their Sunday best,
Like people who have just returned
   From taking a much-needed rest....

They are the fringe of what was rent,
   But if we call that airy roll,
Old loves will answer "Here" and "Here" —
Today — the garment's whole!

For Evening

SHE brushed her brow's fine arches,
   She touched her lips with rouge;
She drew on moon-mist stockings
   And tied on silver shoes.

She slipped into a satin sheath
   That held the orchid's breath;
She dyed her nails a ruby-red,
   And took three grains of death.

The Camel

I FEARED Death so when I was young
The word was aloes on my tongue....
 There was a sentence in a book
 That had a grim and awful look;
Among words to parse and analyze,
It stood in gloom before my eyes:
 "Death is a camel," so it ran,
 "That kneels in front of Everyman."...

When Death came to our street one day,
A frightened child, I ran away.
 From sound of wheels and bow of crepe,
 My young legs, frantic, sought escape.
Beneath our house I crawled away,
With doodlebugs I still could play.
 I scooped a heap of sifting sand
 And felt a doodle in my hand!
It was indeed the nicest way
To hide from Death that wretchéd day.
 No camel now could stoop to steal —
 Why under here he could not kneel!

   ☆ ☆ ☆

No longer young, I face the years
Still captive of those early fears —
 Knowing a camel soon will start
 Across the desert of my heart.

PALE fingers turn the pages
    Of every book I read,
Cool lips still quote the sages
    We learned to love and heed.

The Orchard's white unfolding,
    The day in colored flight,
And beauty's glass I'm holding
    To eyes now shut from sight.

I rouse the sluggish fire
    And when it's quick to blaze
There flames the old desire
    I once knew in a gaze.

I raise no careless finger,
    I draw no casual breath,
But that I know you linger
    Protesting at your death.

The Lost One

A STAR is so high
    And a grave is so low,
Where, oh, where
    Did my loved one go?

I asked the grave
    Where his garments lie,
But grass and granite
    Made no reply.

I begged the star
    To tell where he'd gone,
But proud of shining,
    It twinkled on.

I searched in the valley
    And shouted up-hill,
But echo came back
    Like a sob in the still.

There's no cairn to guide me,
    No wise one to say,
"Here's the road that he took
    On that desolate day."

For living is losing —
    The dead alone know
Why a star is so high
    And a grave is so low.

*T*HE redbird came at morning,
The bluebird came at noon,
But wholly without warning
The dark bird came too soon.

The redbird came for begging,
And settled for a husk,
The bluebird came for singing —
The dark bird brought the dusk.

The bluebird only ate a crumb
And sang for me alone,
The dark bird took my heart away
And left me with a stone.

The Secret Season.

THE SECRET SEASON, The Edwin Markham
Memorial Prize, Judge: Josephine Pinckney, Poetry Society of
Georgia.

THE ORCHARD, The Saturday Review of Literature.

THE DREAMER, The Society Prize, Judge: Daniel
Whitehead Hicky, Poetry Society of Georgia.

THE SIGNAL, Spirit, a Magazine of Poetry.

THESE BARE BRANCHES, Honorable Mention,
Poetry Society of Georgia.

TO A PERFECT HOST, Unpublished.

NOW morning wears the mask of night
    That hides the candor of the sun;
    Wake then upon the furtive dark
        And know day has begun.

    The alien fog creeps in from sea
    With cloudy brow and muffled cloak;
    Grope then along the unseen way
        Until you reach the phantom oak.

    Upon the disappearing path
    Your hushed footfall will not be heard;
    Go then into the hidden house
        Without the whisper of a word.

    Crouch here before the empty hearth
    Where, if he speaks, there will be flame....
    It is the secret season now,—
        But must Love, too, conceal his name?

The Orchard

AND in my orchard joy hangs overlong,
    Enticing none that once was bliss to share.
    The wasps buzz thickly in the sickening air,
    The droppings of the birds are on each rung
    Of the ruined ladder where it leans among
    The sprawling trees, a clumsy waiting stair
    To fruit for which the passer does not care,
    So quickly to young orchards moves the throng.

I should have known that their taste would be fleeting,
    That autumn would come without any delight;
    Say it's a tale much too old for repeating,
    But even the gleaner must come before night.
    Joy's not the best fruit for elderly eating,
    Better by far that it suffer a blight.

$\mathcal{A}$ND then I dreamed,"said Mary, and we were humbly still,
   "Of trees with boughs as pale as clouds tethered on a hill,
   And from this hillside where I stood, as far as eye could see
   Stretched fallow fields of mellow soil and these belong to me.
   I own a meadow wrapped in mist — too lovely to unveil —
   And cattle wading in its pools and they are phantom-pale."

This husbandry of Mary's, this spectral soil she tills
Has cleared the wilderness of night beyond the muted hills;
Yet never once has given from arbor or from field
The long awaited harvest, the much desired yield.

Her orchards know no season but bend beneath their fruit,
Her berries never pelted pail — they wax upon the root.
Her grain is never gathered — it stands in ghostly sheaves,
Her deer are never hunted but peer from silver leaves....

   Still fearful of the product, the hounds' exultant bay,
   She counts her eerie acres — resentful of the day.

The Signal

FAR out beyond this shorebound sea
A fleeting symbol beckons me.
Too dimly seen to reckon shape,
I yearn to know it yet escape
With rapid strokes until I reach
The lap of the maternal beach.

Late sun has haloed shore and people
Where some children build a steeple;
Where, lulled by summer's drowsy hand,
The quick are lying in the sand.
In such bright air how dull to heed
A phantom sign one cannot read!

Like notes of love to Heaven's door
The gulls forsake the shrinking shore;
And day departs, and so do we,
Remarking far-off sails at sea,
Remarking cottage lights now bloom
As stemless blossoms in the gloom.

So, like a known bird in the hand,
Security lies on the land,
And steadfast stars appear and yet,
A fleeting thing I can't forget—
I can't forget there came to me
A desperate signal from the sea
And I denied that it could be!

*N*EVER mating birds or nests
    Share the heart of me —
Not the leafy lattice mine
    But the tattered tree.

Never green rains rush to prick
    These bare branches into bud,
Autumn rains that strike and smart
    Freeze the eager blood.

Seldom does the roving sun
    Touch this bleakness with his lips;
Not for me the brimming boughs
    But the icy whips.

To a perfect host

NOW that my bags are almost packed
With what has gone before,
And soon the motor will await
My presence at the door —

I want to take this chance to say
That ever since my birth
I've relished every minute
I lived upon Your earth.

I've loved Your sunlight on my limbs,
Your moonlight in my veins,
The colors of Your seasons,
The freedom of Your plains.

Your nights have been almost divine,
Yes, indiscreetly so!
And when I think about Your days,
I do not want to go...

Forgive me if I don't convey
One-tenth of my delight —
A bread-and-butter note I find
Is always hard to write!

In an upper room beyond

ROOMS, Columbia Poetry, Columbia University Press.

HE IS NOT HERE, Anthology of Verse, Poetry Society of Georgia.

NINETEEN FORTY-THREE, Year Book, Poetry Society of Georgia.

THE STOREHOUSE, Critics Prize, Poetry Society of Georgia.